Y0-BCO-479

What Research Says to the Teacher

Research Implications for Writing in the Content Areas

by Joanne M. Yates

nea PROFESSIONAL LIBRARY
National Education Association
Washington, D.C.

The Author

Joanne M. Yates is in Special Education, Napa County Schools, California. She is the coauthor (with Stephen N. Tchudi) of *Teaching Writing in the Content Areas: Senior High School,* published by NEA.

Printing History:

First Printing: September 1983
Second Printing: March 1985

Note

The opinions expressed in this publication should not be construed as representing the policy or position of the National Education Association. Materials published as part of the What Research Says to the Teacher series are intended to be discussion documents for teachers who are concerned with specialized interests of the profession.

Library of Congress Cataloging in Publication Data

Yates, Joanne Mueller.
  Research implications for writing in the content areas.

  Bibliography: p.
  1. Language arts. 2. English language—Study and teaching. 3. Curriculum planning. 4. Educational research. I. Title.
LB1576.Y37 1983 808'.042'07 83-13374
ISBN 0-8106-1060-4

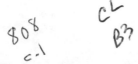

CONTENTS

HISTORICAL OVERVIEW AND RESEARCH FINDINGS

Writing across the curriculum is an old-but-new idea that has evolved from the progressive philosophy of the educator/philosopher John Dewey. Like his colleagues G. Stanley Hall and William Heard Kilpatrick, Dewey hoped to reform education by making it more useful and by giving students an active role in their own learning (4).* Under the influence of progressivism, many schools in the twenties, thirties, and forties developed an interdisciplinary, project-oriented or experience-centered curriculum, encouraging community interest and offering alternatives to traditional academic courses. Students were asked to take part in what was happening around them—writing plays on social and political issues, discussing environmental concerns, presenting story hours to the community, and forming reading clubs to examine works more closely related to their own experiences and concerns (4, 133). Many English and subject-matter classrooms became places where students could pursue their own interests, broaden their experiences, analyze and solve problems, and use writing and reading as an integral part of learning.

Although progressive education gained broad acceptance, many educators, parents, and students felt it lacked intellectual rigor (4), and in the fifties Dewey's ideas fell out of favor. Then, when the United States failed to win the race to launch the first space satellite, Dewey and the progressives were blamed (44, 142). Consequently, traditional educational practices replaced the methods and ideas of the experience curricula: math and science enjoyed government funding and interest, and the study of English lost whatever interdisciplinary flavor it had acquired. Teachers became academic specialists, teaching in tight 50-minute blocks and paying little attention to the interrelationship of subjects.

Throughout the sixties and seventies, education—especially the teaching of reading and writing—continued to be scrutinized by the public (8, 142). In 1974, the Educational Testing Service issued the news that SAT verbal scores had declined 40 points in ten years. This led to a decade of careful examination of reading and writing skills, culminating in the 1983 report of the National Commission on Excellence in Education, *A Nation at Risk* (U.S.

* Numbers in parentheses appearing in the text refer to the Bibliography beginning on page 26.

4

Department of Education). These studies fueled a back-to-basics movement that called for more rigorous rote and drills in isolated skills. There was, however, another influential movement, sparked by the work and practices of James Britton (26) and John Dixon (42). Certain educators (John Holt, Paul Goodman, Daniel Fader, Jonathan Kozol, and Herbert Kohl) advocated greater freedom to work and learn in the classrooms (4; 8, pp. 51–62).

Amidst this foment, Dewey's concerns and the ideas of the progressives resurfaced in a movement called "writing across the curriculum." Teachers in Great Britain and the United States, echoing the progressive concern for a more practical, experience-oriented curriculum, saw interdisciplinary studies as a way to break down the artificial boundaries between subject areas (26, 39, 163). They found that learning logs, journals, and projects such as student-written (and published) newspapers, readers, and a host of other activities provided opportunities for lively interaction between learner and subject. Even more encouraging, for the first time, extensive studies done by teachers in their schools, as well as hard scientific data, confirmed that language learning and experience are at the heart of education (30, 34, 54, 121, 141).

Just what does this mean for teachers? The implications are that (1) instruction should be based on the personal and linguistic growth of the child rather than on the mastery of facts or concepts in particular disciplines; and (2) subject areas should be used to provide students with the new experiences they need to broaden their knowledge. In other words, researchers and educators propose a teaching philosophy and approach based on the concept of *learning by doing* (7, 8, 26, 36, 42, 132).

Therefore, much more talking, writing, and reading should take place in the classroom in order to enhance learning and to explore course content. For example, studies show that talking is a vital act in the learning process because it permits children to discuss what is happening or has happened to them (7, 11, 53). A child may want to talk about the cat that followed her to school that was run over and killed in the street, in order to understand the occurrence and to share the small tragedy with others. Another student may come to class eager to tell classmates about a story he's read or about a visit to his grandparents. Exchanging ideas and giving shape and meaning to experiences through talking is one way children establish relationships between people, events, and experiences (11).

Writing provides the same opportunities: ". . . children learn by writing. By learn I mean above all this process by which they shape their experience in order to make it available to themselves to learn from" (53, p. 28). It is important, then, to see writing as a process of learning or understanding, and not only as a means for feeding back information that "should have been learned" (as most tests or book reports use it). For example, when students consider social or ethical issues involved in genetic engineering, they not only recall information they are getting in class, but they must also reflect on it, make connections with their own experiences and ideas, and begin to imagine and speculate how that information may affect their own world (108, pp. 63–96). This kind of writing becomes a conscious exploration of subject matter because students must make assertions and applications using the material at hand (121).

Research shows that reading is another means for expanding the experiences of students through language (36, 59, 93, 133). Reading exposes the child to someone else's ideas or representation of the world and those ideas add to the child's experience and knowledge (53, pp. 49–53). Thus, teachers using a language-centered curriculum encourage students to become involved in their reading and actively respond to the ideas, rather than focus on close textual analysis, genre study, literary periods, and other more technical concerns. For example, a fourth grade class reading about whales is introduced to a view of sea and mammal life that is new to them. These fresh ideas not only enrich their knowledge but can also bring them to an understanding of their own place in the world (11, pp. 36–51). This kind of reading is not the passive act of picking up information to be reused later, but rather a way for students to expand their world, modify their ideas, and understand their own experiences in relation to those of others.

A number of educators and researchers in England and the United States who have been using these principles in the classroom have documented the results in careful studies over the last 20 years (87, 102). In 1971, Janet Emig published a study on the composing processes of twelfth graders showing that no single writing process existed and that writing was a circular as well as a linear act (48). Other research on the writing process followed focusing on specific stages and influences. Donald Graves closely examined the methods seventh graders used to compose and the effect of the social environment on their work (63). Mina Shaughnessy studied the patterns of errors in the compositions of college freshmen to determine the role error played in writing (140). And

Donald Murray focused on revision in order to examine its importance in the process (115, 116). All these studies are considered part of the fields of discourse analysis, psycho- and sociolinguistics, and composition research.

Moreover, these studies have been supported by other kinds of research. In the area of child language acquisition, investigators have found that children must undergo a lengthy period of exposure to a variety of language experiences before they are ready to speak. Within months of their birth, infants begin to formulate concepts and hypotheses about how language works: they break it down to its simplest parts and then develop rules that help them put it back together (113). Essential to this process is error-making, which provides children with the opportunity to test out their theories and modify them as needed. And because of individual learning styles, the length of time needed to learn to speak varies in each child as do the methods each one uses to analyze language (54, 113).

Data collected in brain research amplifies these findings. The majority of work in this field over the last 150 years has concentrated on language processing and learning. Karl Wernicke and Paul Broca were the first to identify the language areas of the brain: Wernicke located the area where information is given meaning and Broca discovered the area where ideas acquire proper grammatical and articulation patterns (61). Recent studies confirm their findings and moreover show that long-term learning takes place when all the language areas (audio and visual as well) are involved in processing, interpreting, and storing information (30, 73, 94). Experiments carried out during neurosurgery also reveal that the brain parses sentences as soon as the eye registers the words it reads: verbs travel along one set of neural pathways, while prepositions and nouns use different routes. These pathways are established long before the person ever sees a grammar text (14). Although these studies cannot crack the codes and patterns used by the brain to learn, they conclude that the brain is a very creative problem solver that relies on error and confusion as a means for hypothesizing and understanding (73, 88).

The case studies and careful practical research done by people such as Britton, Emig, Graves, Shaughnessy, Murray, and many others are showing that the language-centered and experience-oriented approaches work in the classroom. At the same time, the scientific, clinical data is helping to explain why. The writing-across-the-curriculum movement with its interdisciplinary emphasis is especially compatible with these findings and implications; for this reason it is gaining interest and support from many educators (13, 68, 74, 96, 106, 139, 156).

The following general conclusions can help teachers use writing more effectively in the classroom.

1. *Writing is tied to the other language acts.*

Writing is reinforced by talking, listening, and reading. Incorporating these acts into the learning process helps students test and compare their ideas in order to communicate more effectively. Because all students learn differently and at different rates, using all the language acts in writing enables them to find and develop the techniques more compatible with their learning styles (7, 10, 29, 83, 92).

2. *Writing is learned holistically.*

Like talking, writing is learned by working on whole problems rather than on isolated skills. Holistic learning involves creative problem solving, repetition, hypothesis formation, testing and error-making. Therefore, providing frequent opportunities and different kinds of assignments helps students learn to write (11, 22, 54, 85).

3. *Writing is a process.*

All writers move through many stages, from conceiving an idea to completing a final draft; and often they must go through these stages several times to rewrite and clarify their ideas. However, there is no one process or set of strategies that all writers use. Therefore, teachers should present a variety of methods that students can use for each stage and to help them develop their own approaches to the writing process (31, 46, 48, 120, 121).

4. *Writing is communication.*

Like speech, writing carries ideas from one person to another, has a distinct purpose and audience, and is based on meaning. Therefore, students need to develop a sense of audience and purpose, and see writing as a relevant act that occurs between themselves and their classroom or society (11, 27, 29, 54, 116).

ADAPTING THE APPROACH

Many content-area teachers may feel uncomfortable in the role of "writing/reading" teacher, but they should be relieved by the fact that writing or reading cannot be "taught." Students learn to write by writing; they learn to read by reading (20, 22, 24, 26, 46, 83). Yet there are a number of ways for teachers to promote more language activities to help students learn without becoming reading and writing specialists. Furthermore, incorporating more writing, reading, and talking into a class does not mean that content-area teachers have to grade briefcase-loads of papers in addition to their other responsibilities. The following suggestions, based on classroom experience, will help adapt interdisciplinary and language-based approaches to any subject area.

Course Design

1. *Thematic Content*

Many teachers advocate organizing course content around central ideas or themes to give language assignments direction, focus, and purpose (2, 35, 45, 62, 72, 83, 86, 90, 129, 143, 155). The chart on the following pages from *The ABC's of Literacy* (83) provides general themes and topics that can be adapted to any classroom or discipline.

Generally, it is easier to design a more coherent, thematic curriculum in an elementary school where students spend the day primarily with one teacher and in one room. For example, the general theme of social and natural environment is especially appropriate for grade school students because they are so actively involved in understanding what is going on around them. Topics related to this theme include community history, weather, local geography, populations and cultural heritages, regional wildlife, local economy, and sports. Possible related projects are community history books or pamphlets, maps, tourist guides, almanacs, weather forecasting, markets or fairs, class readers of creative writing, nature hikes, art and photo exhibits, musicals, dramas, family histories, and recipe books.

Despite the division of subjects and the emphasis on skills testing and teaching in upper grades, numerous language activities and interdisciplinary approaches can still be incorporated into the junior and senior high school curriculum. By using the themes suggested on the following chart, teachers can dovetail required course material with projects that expand students' interest and knowledge of the disciplines.

2. *The Writing Process*

Teachers find that using the writing process not only improves students' work, but gives teachers a more active role in their

A Model Curriculum for English*

	UNITS/TOPICS/COURSES	READING	COMPOSITION
ELEMENTARY YEARS	A full range of experiences make up the "curriculum" of the school. Subjects for language work range from field trips to personal experiences to school subjects.	Wide reading and use of print and non-print media. Free reading, picture books, being read to, listening to recorded literature. Informal book talks with teachers or librarians.	Equally free writing, story-telling, sharing show and tell. Playing language games. Giving dictation. Improvised drama, charades, panto-mime.
JUNIOR HIGH/ MIDDLE SCHOOLS A. *Vicarious Experience*	Topics: *The World Around Us, Sounds and Sights, Fire and Ice, Snakes, Hunting, Our Town, Sports Animals, Faraway Places, Travel, Truth Is Stranger Than Fiction.*	Fiction and nonfiction dealing with the natural world, with an emphasis on the exciting and adventuresome, as well as things close to home.	Sensory writing, writing about observations, haiku poetry, personal narratives, keeping diaries.
B. *Fantasy Adventure*	*High Adventure, Romance, Survival, The Supernatural, Unknown Worlds, Detectives, Science Fiction, Ghouls and Goblins.*	Much action-packed fiction. Sci fi, detectives, mystery, adventure, horror, Hardy Boys stories, Nancy Drew, Alfred Hitchcock.	Writing of the same—tales of adventure, mystery, horror, intrigue. Improvised and scripted drama of horror, adventure, romance. Roleplaying: "If I were...."
C. *Seeing Oneself*	*Who Am I?, Coming of Age, Loneliness, Dreams and Visions, Autobiographies, Personal Puzzles and Problems.*	All genres: poetry, prose, essays, films, and video dealing with identity. Especially stories by and about young people.	Personal and introspective writing: journals, diaries, personal narratives, contemplative poetry, personal poetry, values clarifying roleplay.
SENIOR HIGH SCHOOL A. *Human Relationships*	*Conflicts, Family Relationships, Rebellion, Friends and Enemies, Youth and Age, Making Connections with Others.*	Increasing use of adult as well as young adult literature. Literary discussion focuses on characters and their interaction. While some books describe peer	Introspective writing, with an increased emphasis on sharing thoughts in public. Dramatic improvisations on human problems. Conscious efforts to improve group

			writing remain important, students can move into a full range of public discourse, including creative essays, formal letters, discussion, debate, analysis.
	Nature, Youth, Minorities, Schooling, Death and Dying, Hero/Anti-Hero, Might and Right, Future Shock, Utopian Visions, Prophecy.	or literature—juvenile and adult—is available to students. Many opportunities exist for the teacher to move beyond "pure" literature into magazines, newspapers, and the like.	
C. *Learning and Knowing*	Issues, problems, moral concerns. Plus increasing connections with exploring and knowing in other disciplines; e.g., chemistry, anthropology, physics.	The full resources of the library should be made available. In addition, students can learn to "read" and gain information through media, interviews, research, and experimentation.	"Research" can be written in many forms: essay, term paper, poem, story, drama. The full range should be explored.
D. *Aesthetic Experience*		As appropriate to the subject, including contemporary and classic fiction and nonfiction, media resources, magazines and journal articles, elementary critical articles. Discussion begins with exploration of the text and the reader's responses, then moves toward informal critical analysis. The connections between personal response and objective criticism are explored in depth.	The focus of composition will naturally tend to emphasize the analytical and critical—writing about literature. However, the thrust toward personal, introspective, and creative writing can and should continue, lest the program become strictly "academic." Further, the students' own writing is appropriately subject to more formal critical analysis. Drama in English will increasingly focus on presentation, of student writing as well as literature, through readers' theatre, plays, etc.
History/Culture	*Civil War Literature, The Literature of the Twenties, The American Revolution, Ethnic Literature, Literature of East and West.*		
Genre	*Folklore, Mythology, Science Fiction, The Lyric, Contemporary Poetry, Classic Plays, The Western, The Spy Novel, Television Novels.*		
Theme	*Existentialism, Politics in Literature, Frontiers, Courage, The Young Person in Literature, American Myths and Dreams.*		

* From *The ABC's of Literacy* by Stephen N. Judy (New York: Oxford University Press, 1980), pp. 222–23.
© 1980 by Oxford University Press, Inc. Reprinted by permission.

students' learning (20, 31, 46, 120). Writing in stages allows students (a) to explore a subject or idea in order to find what they want to discuss (prewriting or invention); (b) to write and then reexamine their ideas (revision); (c) to test out or rehearse their ideas with classmates or friends (peer-evaluation or editing); and (d) to concentrate on style and correctness (rewriting and copyediting). Many of these stages can be started at home and continued during class where teachers can spot check writing and make suggestions or corrections as students work.

3. *Projects for Public Presentation*

Provisions for class projects such as publications and presentations in course units reinforce the idea that good writing must communicate (29, 54, 56, 62, 116). Having an audience to write for helps students see why their work should be interesting, well developed, organized, and clearly written. Furthermore, these projects give students more motivation to communicate because they are involved in expressing ideas that are important to them.

Language Activities

1. *Journals*

Journals, reading notes, or learning logs are among the easiest and most successful assignments that can be added to any curriculum (20, 46, 58, 59, 74, 81, 106). They are especially important in the learning process because they afford students the opportunity to describe and explore their own experiences and to record their opinions, impressions, insights, questions, musing, feelings, or interpretations regarding class topics, discussion, or readings. Because the purpose of the journal (or learning or reading log) is to express ideas, most teachers do not grade or correct them, nor do they require students to focus on neatness, penmanship, spelling, or grammar. Such considerations can be attended to in formal writing projects that go through several stages and drafts before becoming final projects ready for public reading or presentation.

Furthermore, journals allow for regular and sustained work which is crucial in developing writing abilities. Many teachers provide enough time and motivation for regular writing practice by (a) setting aside 10 minutes of class time for writing several times a week, (b) setting a minimum number of pages to be completed each week, (c) assigning opened-ended questions related to class subjects that encourage students to view material from varied perspectives, or (d) using surveys or questionnaires as a source of topics to draw out and capitalize on students' experiences and interests.

2. *Assignment Alternatives*

Research suggests that it is important to build in alternative projects or language activities when planning course units or assignments (21, 28, 52, 67, 70, 75, 83, 85, 107, 155, 156, 161). For example, if students are studying the planets, they need not give reports or complete fill-in-the-blank tests to learn and use course material. They can write science-fiction short stories; conduct imaginary interviews with extraterrestial beings; present a minidocudrama on the treatment of Galileo because of his revolutionary ideas; or design space communities where their children or grandchildren may live someday.

Everyone learns in different ways and has varying interests; by providing alternative assignments, teachers allow more students to find their own connections to course material. The following list of language activities is taken from the materials cited in the bibliography for this section; they can be applied to almost any assignment or topic.

Writing: Scripts for dramas, TV or radio productions, interviews
Science, detective, historical, romantic, adolescent, or juvenile fiction
Poetry
Bumper stickers/slogans
Sequels
Graffiti walls
Advertisements
Letters
Imaginary diaries/journals of fictional or real characters
Recipe books, folk medicine collections, family histories and trees
Community tourist guides/historical pamphlets
Newspapers/newsletters
Resumes, job descriptions, business reports
Health/exercise guides
How-to/factual or statistical collections (such as the *Guinness Book of Records*, *Old Farmer's Almanac*, or *Ripley's Believe It or Not*)

13

Talking/	Book talks/reviews
Media:	Reading/fan clubs
	Dramatizations of readings or events/improvisations
	Panels
	Debates
	Radio productions (radio-reader, serializations, documentaries, broadcasts, musicals)
	Interviews
	TV productions (soaps, historical dramas, news broadcasts, sit-coms, commercials)
	Outside speakers
	Film/slide presentations
	Videotapes
	Field trips
Art:	Photo/drawing/sculpture exhibits
	Rubbings/leaf prints
	Cartoon collections/comic strips
	Scale models of communities, spaceships, cars, geographical locations, natural wonders
	Mobiles
	Collages
	Maps
	Flip books
	Games

3. *Reading Experience*

Teachers can promote more reading activities by supplementing textbook assignments with young adult trade books, paperbacks, magazines, newspapers, and biographies of major figures in their discipline. Asking students to bring in clippings, books, and articles that they find also encourages their involvement in class topics (12, 47, 77, 86, 127, 138).

In addition, research suggests that teachers should encourage students to respond to ideas and concepts, help them relate course content to their own experiences, and have them produce their own texts for class (24, 29, 51, 85, 86, 133).

Grading and Evaluation

Studies show that careful teacher correction and grading of compositions does little to improve student writing (82, 101, 102, 140, 160). What is important is that students write more often.

Another way to ease the pressure of grading and evaluation is to use the writing process in class (24, 46, 131). With this approach teachers can help students solve writing problems while they write rather than comment on errors or problems after they hand in the papers. During the drafting, revising, and rewriting stages, students also have several opportunities to iron out problems. Moreover, studies show that once students have a clearer understanding of their ideas, they generally make fewer grammatical and spelling errors in their work. (And those that remain can be caught and corrected in copyediting sessions when teachers and classmates can spot check and proofread work.)

The following guide is a commonsense list of suggestions developed to help those not trained as writing teachers to evaluate papers (110, p. 26):

1. Give positive feedback whenever possible; point out strengths as well as weaknesses.

2. Use personal conferences for difficult or sensitive problems.

3. Respond to specific problems with specific suggestions for improvement wherever possible.

4. Do not "grade" early drafts; reserve such judgment for final drafts.

5. Create sample "self-critique" sheets to help students guide themselves.

6. Give students some responsibility for evaluating each other's work.

WHAT TEACHERS ARE DOING

The last section of this publication is divided into the following subject areas: English, foreign language/bilingual education, history/social science, and science/math. Each area contains critiques of several articles written by teachers who describe what they are doing to incorporate more language and interdisciplinary activities into their classrooms. Although some of the selections concentrate on themes or topics rather than on specific assignments, the list of writing, talking, and art projects on the preceding pages provides a great many ideas for assignments that can be used to explore thematic content.

English

The potential for interdisciplinary study in the English classroom is unlimited. Students and teachers can investigate any subject in the humanities or sciences to gain an understanding of what has gone on in the past, to interpret the present, or to make predictions about the future. Because of this flexibility and multidimensional character, English departments can also take an active role in promoting a schoolwide program of writing across the curriculum by disseminating research and offering guidance to other teachers (145).

The following descriptions show how some teachers use other disciplines to promote reading and writing in English courses.

1. Because of their predominant humanities background, some English teachers are reluctant to approach science topics in their classrooms. However, many political and social issues connected to science make appropriate and stimulating subjects (45, 47). Among these are the environment, the space program, genetic engineering, the advent of computers, video games and word processors, energy alternatives, and the modern diet (76). After investigating these topics, students can present their findings and conclusions in debates, letters, taped interviews, panels or science fairs, slide shows, or documentaries (47).

Science writing in the English class can also be done in journals that record observations of natural phenomena (11, pp. 52–69). Students in a rural school in England kept copious notebooks on their experiences with gardening and raising animals, their observations of the seasons and the accompanying changes, as well as observations of the creatures brought to class by fellow students. Later these notebooks became a valuable resource for ideas and descriptions that were used for poetry, paintings, drawings, and other creative projects.

2. Second graders in a Michigan school are citizens of the town of "Betterburg" where they participate in community activities and governance (56). Their town is also a site for all types of language work. Students have compiled a town history and drawn detailed maps depicting major features and locations. They use newscasts and summaries to report current events. Some students work on manuscripts for class publication. And all the "citizens" are kept busy in reading groups or working individually on worksheets, letters, or creative writing projects.

16

In establishing their town, students also needed to contact local and state government officials for guidance in writing their laws and enforcement policies. Since Betterburg's start, commerce has grown; students now sell goods within their community as well as to the "neighboring" town of Haslett. Not only has Betterburg stimulated and helped students develop their writing and reading abilities, it has made education more immediate and meaningful.

3. Popular culture is another natural interdisciplinary topic (85). It enriches students' understanding of America and Americans and helps them better understand their own tastes and values. Materials for units are readily available—paperbacks, magazines, newspapers, television, radio, music, films, and art—and the possibilities for projects almost limitless.

For a fresh view of history, students can examine one period or day (a person's birthday, Lindbergh's landing in Paris, a particular war event) and find out which fads, ideas, customs, literature, music, philosophies, or films were current at that time. Another approach is looking at collections: what Americana do people collect and why?

Still another possibility is studying genres. Students can read (and write) westerns, gothic romances, horror stories, detective and spy stories, science fiction, and comics to discover what makes them so popular and what they have to say about America. They can also focus on music (singers, trends, groups, songs, or periods), television (soap operas, situation comedies, dramas, commercials, or news reporting), movies (film noir, teenage horror, science fiction, westerns, mysteries, or romantic comedies), and art (artists, trends, philosophies, or specific works and periods).

4. "Writing about the job market, including desirable skills and procedures, appears to be an important—and legitimate—means of stimulating student writing." (104, p. 43) Some high school students are developing their reading, writing, and speaking abilities by investigating what employers expect from them. Not only do students practice cover letters and resumes, but they—

a. Write and practice interviews.
b. Explore the social and economic payoff of using standard English.
c. Write reports on the skills needed for different jobs.
d. Interview managers, factory workers, professionals about job requirements and demands.

e. Maintain journals about their experiences.

f. Write autobiographies emphasizing employment experience.

g. Write plays, radio, or TV scripts set in job situations.

h. Write advertisements and commercials.

i. Research the economy and job market.

j. Practice keeping checking accounts and establishing charge accounts.

Such activities sharpen and develop students' language abilities, and prepare them for future concerns as well.

History and Social Science

These disciplines offer students and teachers the chance to look at subjects from historical and social perspectives, inviting them to interpret events, rather than just know facts (147). Writing and talking about people, places, and events are ways of making history and social science alive and meaningful because they allow students to discover relationships between past and present, and to probe issues that affect their lives.

1. Using local history is one means for developing students' abilities to observe the world (32). Students in an Amherst (Massachusetts) high school began their local history projects by imagining what it was like to live in the town during the nineteenth century. They visited local museums; went to private homes and government buildings to observe colonial architecture; studied paintings, delved into short stories, poetry, plays and novels; listened to folk music; and watched selected films about colonial life to develop a more intimate feeling for the period.

Class projects that evolved from their work included pasteboard models of early New England buildings and a replica of early Amherst, a colonial dinner based on recipe books from the period, and journals in which students imagined themselves to be historical characters living in 1778 and later in the 1830s. Showing these projects to others gave students real motivation for sharing their discoveries about Amherst's past.

2. Another important but often overlooked source of inter- disciplinary language projects in history and social science is micofilmed newspapers. One teacher used the *Virginia Gazette* from the early 1700s to explore the idea of news and the role of newspapers in society (138). Examining and discussing the stories

in class led to a number of topics for further student research: Virginia society (men, women and children, entertainment, contemporary lifestyles, science and medicine, Indian life, crime, and justice); slavery; economic life (British policy, tobacco trade, plantation life); religion; world events; political events; and political life.

3. Letterwriting in a government course is a method used by two teachers (one from a suburban, the other from an inner-city school) to help students become more informed, thoughtful citizens who were aware of certain social and political issues in their community (11, pp. 175–95).

The project started as an option: suburban students could write to a pen pal in an urban school, and inner-city students could write to them. Once students received their first mail, even the most reluctant writers wanted to join in. The first letter was an introduction in which students described themselves, their school, and communities. In later correspondence, students started to develop their relationships—writing about their lifestyles, asking and answering questions, beginning to share important aspects of their lives, giving advice on personal problems, and discussing different societal issues that affected them, especially the topic of prejudice. The issues raised in the letters turned into important class discussions where students could talk about their feelings and ideas on race, class, and cultural differences.

In a required government class whose members are usually uninterested in the political world, letterwriting provided personal experiences that helped students define for themselves the concepts of democracy, equality, and justice.

4. News broadcasting was one way a California high school improved students' writing and speaking skills and made social studies a very timely subject (103). The project was writing and producing a complete news program for a local television station. To do this, students had to learn the specialized language of news production, watch network news carefully to discover the elements necessary for a successful program, learn to use videotape equipment, select story ideas, interview and film their subjects, write and edit news copy, plan the show, and present their stories to the public. It was a demanding program, but one that students enjoyed and worked hard at in order to become good reporters and technicians.

Even though all schools do not have the funds or resources to present a TV news program, many of the activities described in this article can be used for preparing shorter broadcasts on local radio, school public address systems, or class tape recorders. Written work can be collected in newsletters or newspapers and can feature local personalities or important issues and events.

5. Writing about science is another approach especially suitable for history or social science courses. In an age when people are beginning to mistrust science and technology, it is most important to evaluate and explain the role science plays in everyone's life (150). Using a historical or social perspective allows students to do so. Furthermore, integrating these disciplines through different language activities develops student abilities to define problems, develop hypotheses, test their ideas against research and observations, develop conclusions, and make generalizations and evaluations. Areas for investigations include pollution, energy alternatives, genetic engineering, euthanasia, cancer and space research, endangered species, food additives, transportation, urban planning.

Foreign Languages/Bilingual Education

Studies predict that more emphasis in foreign language teaching will be placed on practical use and international understanding (23). This means that students should be exposed to teaching techniques that are based on recent research in language acquisition (54, 119), and that more time should be devoted to interdisciplinary topics that explore culture (23, 149). Already many bilingual, immersion, and FLES (Foreign Language in the Elementary School) programs show this research and interest in culture providing new stimulus for writing, talking, and learning.

1. The medieval epic, *Chanson de Roland,* was used in a French bilingual program in Cincinnati to broaden and enliven a social studies unit (127). The children were most interested in the conflicts between good and evil in the epic because of their own questions concerning right and wrong. They also discussed the ideas of friendship, loyalty, bravery, and pride—important aspects of life in either medieval France or twentieth century America. Students listened to the storyteller, imagining themselves seated around a castle fireplace on a wintry night. After the readings, they discussed the ideas and events described in the poem, imagined locales and studied geography, practiced medieval boasts and

insults, dramatized certain passages, practiced writing medieval script, and played word games based on new vocabulary.

As this study and others show (77), literature of other countries, either in the original language or in translation, offers a number of topics and projects for social studies, English, or foreign language classes (149).

2. Some foreign language teachers are using popular songs in their classroom to develop students' listening comprehension, vocabulary, grammar, conversation, and composition abilities, in addition to exploring the culture and history the music represents (2). After listening to and understanding the lyrics, students use new and known vocabulary to devise their own word games. These involve writing short definitions or learning homonyms, synonyms, or antonyms. Songs with story lines or philosophical questions work well to stimulate conversations and writing. Students can also narrate, write, or act out stories or issues, or invent dialogues or more detailed lyrics that develop the author's ideas or their own interpretations. Many songs also present social messages about war, friendship, ecology, progress, and prejudice. Examining these issues and other nations' methods of dealing with them gives students fresh insights on culture, heritage, and international relations.

3. Some bilingual programs focus on folklore to develop language because it taps students' knowledge of culture and history; gives them greater confidence and motivation for reading, writing, and talking; and offers a limitless array of subjects for projects (62). Students can begin folklore units by interviewing family and friends to collect proverbs, riddles, jokes, myths, legends, rhymes, poetry, songs, and ballads. This initial research can lead to discussions on cultural superstitions, traditions, customs and beliefs, or to studies on regional dance, art, drama, literature, and cuisine. Students can develop their knowledge of these subjects by organizing festivals that incorporate dancing, foods, and handicrafts; acting out legends, myths, and poetry, or performing ballads; compiling recipe books, folk medicine remedies, joke and riddle books; or incorporating holiday celebrations and customs into classroom activities.

As research suggests, bringing folklore into bilingual or foreign language classes is especially useful in promoting understanding and appreciation of other cultures because it allows students to view the heritage of others as well as to examine their own.

4. Helping students who speak English as a second language read and write is a growing concern in the schools. One teacher in a San Diego inner-city school used a camera and the local community to provide the tools for purposeful learning (11, pp. 77–80). Students began this program by taking photographs of people or things that were important in their lives and discussing them in class. They not only explained the significance of the shots, but they also discussed the success of their work—whether or not each photograph was interesting to other members of the class and its purpose clear. These initial projects and discussions evolved into stories, a guidebook of the school for new students, a 25-page book about the Chicano clinic, class activity books, displays, exhibits, interviews, and games. Eventually, students even improvised a sound studio for taping their stories and interviews. Their last project for the year was writing career pamphlets based on interviews with people who worked in their community.

Not only did these projects give these ESL students more power and facility in English, but they helped them develop and establish a positive self-image in their community—an important facet in language learning and development (114).

Science and Mathematics

Bringing writing to these areas is especially important in today's society because of the mutual lack of understanding between the humanities and the sciences (47). Moreover, math and science teachers are finding that using more written and oral projects sparks greater interest and learning in their classrooms (151). And research shows that science activities count, especially for disadvantaged students (25).

1. Teachers can devise a number of language-science activities for students as take-home projects that involve their families and that reinforce the position of science in all their lives (107). For example, to help students understand more about their bodies, growth, and the importance of nutrition, have them list the physical characteristics of relatives, keep journals of foods they eat, devise games based on food groups, or write (or invent) alternative recipes to junk-food diets. To observe plant and animal life, have students map their backyards or neighborhoods, identifying the homes of certain plants or animals, do natural bark rubbings, start leaf or rock collections; or lie under a tree to observe all the activity going on in the tree's world. Sorting and grouping is the

first step in learning to classify. To develop this ability, students can make texture collections of soft, rough, or smooth things; collect rubbings of different items inside or outside the home; or start rock, leaf, flower, insect, or butterfly collections.

2. Some teachers are capitalizing on their students' interest in Buck Rogers and *Star Wars* to study the solar system and to develop their language abilities (78). Projects include designing settlements for earthlings on different planets, developing ways to harness solar energy, debating nuclear energy versus alternative energy sources, imagining life forms that can survive on other planets, writing science fiction stories, listening to music that depicts planets or life in outer space, and then writing poetry, dramatizing life in a space capsule, or portraying ideas about the universe through drawings or paintings.

3. A fourth-grade class in an elementary school whose science program emphasizes wildlife and natural history decided to do a detailed study of marine life, focusing specifically on whales (11, pp. 36–51). Because of their location in northern California, the students were able to view gray whales migrating south and visit a marine aquarium to observe a killer whale. Each day the teacher read from a book pertinent to their interest on whales, and everyone collected and shared materials, wrote journals to record their discoveries and insights, and kept notebooks to chronicle information. The last field trip was a visit to the local pool, and although it was February, students went into the water to imagine what it was like to be a whale. They came out of the water with a greater understanding of how blubber protects and insulates whales, how they breathe, and what it must be like to spend all one's life in water. Eventually, they compiled their research, experiences, and insights for a book about whales written by children for children.

4. Many math teachers are discovering that incorporating more writing, reading, talking, and listening into the classroom is making abstract concepts more accessible to students (11, pp. 123–34). One method is to require students to keep learning logs or journals. The logs serve as notebooks where students write explanations and examples given in class, and record their questions, confusions, interpretations, suggestions, and criticisms regarding class material and teaching methods. In turn, the teacher uses this information to spot problems, to identify students who need extra help, or to modify or amplify teaching materials. Other writing activities

involve giving and responding to accurate directions for building objects with Cuisenaire rods. First students work in small groups, observing others and discussing their projects; then they work individually, building and next describing their projects in writing. In this way they develop their abilities to write more accurate descriptions of mathematical formulas and to read mathematics later in the course or in more advanced classes.

5. Compound growth is a source of problems that involve mathematical calculations and different language activities (114). Students can work on problems concerning monetary inflation, lending, borrowing, payments, investing, population studies, and radioactive decay. They can present their learning to classmates in a number of ways—giving investment tips to working people who can save $25 each pay period or to teenagers saving for a car, college education, or summer trips, for example. Students can also study inflation rates and predict the prices of items in five or ten years; or they can work out plans for people who want to buy a house, compiling information about down payments, amortization rates, and household budgets. Population growth or radioactive decay are other subjects that provide practice and learning in mathematics. Students can predict population growth and then make generalizations about its effects on local, state, or national economies and programs. By learning to calculate the rate of radioactive decay, students not only learn mathematical concepts and formulas, but they gain another perspective on nuclear waste and on the growing controversy surrounding nuclear power.

6. Other teachers are using the environment coupled with language activities to develop students' mathematical abilities (125). For example, the local community offers an immediate wealth of subjects and projects. Students can make neighborhood maps to learn scale and ratio. They can visit (or write letters to) local factories, businesses, or mines to collect data about energy consumption and production, wages, absenteeism, costs of production and storage, accident rates, and retail costs of goods. Those interested in sports can investigate bodily changes and their meaning after different kinds or degrees of exercise. Or students can concentrate on a favorite sport and keep performance records—shots on goal, percentage of shots made, hitting percentages, times, or compile other statistics for a school or class publication.

Another subject is the home. Students can create the ideal "room" that reflects their personality or that develops a certain atmosphere. The project would involve estimating costs, planning for materials, measuring, and doing comparison shopping. They can then use their research to build scale models. Still another favorite subject of students, nature, helps relate mathematics to their experiences. They can study and collect geometric shapes prevalent in the schoolyard or community park, discuss the idea of symmetry and find examples, learn to measure the circumference of trees and relate it to age, or use shadows to determine the height of trees and buildings.

7. A Texas high school teacher uses forensic medicine and her students' interest in the TV personality Quincy to study chemistry (72). The course begins by discussing the first detective involved in forensic medicine, Sherlock Holmes, and by reviewing basic chemical concepts. Then, in preparation for solving a mystery created by the teacher, students learn to analyze fingerprints, soil samples or trace elements, documents for authenticity, and drugs and poisons. The final problem is to investigate an imaginary crime—with victims, suspects, MO files, descriptions of the crime, and physical evidence such as fingerprints, documents, bits of hair. Everyone prepares a report that analyzes the evidence, proposes the crime sequence, and offers solutions. To conclude this chemistry course, the teacher invites guest speakers from the local police department or the FBI, or arranges a field trip to a crime lab or enforcement agency.

CONCLUSION

As the foregoing activities indicate, many teachers are discovering that writing in the content areas can enhance learning. By incorporating language and interdisciplinary activities into their classrooms, they are also confirming the research findings that language learning and experience are at the heart of education. According to the research, instruction should be based on the individual student's personal and linguistic growth, rather than on the mastery of facts or concepts; and subject areas should be used to provide students with new experiences to help them broaden their knowledge. Writing across the curriculum accomplishes both objectives. In other words, it enables students to learn by doing—to become more involved in their learning.

BIBLIOGRAPHY

In addition to the references cited in the text, this Bibliography contains entries on further research and other subject areas in which writing and interdisciplinary projects have been used. These subjects include geography, physical education and recreation, and health education.

1. Abrams, Kathleen. "Literature and Science: An Interdisciplinary Approach to Environmental Studies." *Current Review* 18 (October 1979): 302–4.
2. Abrate, Jane Halsne. "Pedagogical Applications of the French Popular Song in the Foreign Language Classroom." *Modern Language Journal* 67 (January 1983): 8–12
3. Aitchison, Jean. *The Articulate Mammal: An Introduction to Psycholinguistics*. New York: McGraw-Hill Paperbacks, 1978.
4. Applebee, Arthur N. *Tradition and Reform in the Teaching of English: A History*. Urbana, Ill.: National Council of Teachers of English, 1974.
5. _____; Lehr, Fran; and Auten, Anne. "Learning to Write in the Secondary School: How and Where." *English Journal* 70 (September 1981): 78–82.
6. Arenstein, Walter Allan, and Supple, Ginny King. "Solid Waste: It's Elementary: The Research and Development of Two Environmental Education Programs." *Journal of Environmental Education* (Fall 1981): 3–11
7. Armstrong, Michael. *Closely Observed Children: The Diary of a Primary Classroom*. London: Writers and Readers Publishing Cooperative Society, Ltd., 1980.
8. Bagnall, Nicholas, ed. *New Movements in the Study and Teaching of English*. London: Maurice Temple Smith, Ltd., 1973.
9. Bankie, Brett, "Reliving the Gold Rush: An Outdoor Education Program in the Old West." *Communicator* 10, no. 2 (1979): 20–24
10. Barnes, D.; Britton, James; and Rosen, Harold. *Language, the Learner, and the School*. Middlesex, Eng.: Penguin Books, 1971.
11. Barr, Mary; D'Arcy, Pat; and Healy, Mary K. *What's Going On?* Monclair, N.J.: Boynton/Cook Publishers, 1982.
12. Barrow, Lloyd H., and Salesi, Rosemary A. "Integrating Science Activities Through Literature Webs." *School Science and Mathematics* 82 (January 1982): 65–70.
13. Beck, James P. "Theory and Practice of Interdisciplinary Writing." *English Journal* 69 (February 1980): 28–32.
14. Begley, Sharon, et al. "How the Brain Works." *Newsweek* 101 (February 1983): 40–47.
15. Berger, Patrick, and Page, Lane. "From Laputa to Bio-Ethics." *English Journal* 65 (October 1976): 52–54.
16. Berkovits, Annette, and Greenblat, Esther. "Armadillos, Boatbills, and Crocodiles." *Outdoor Communicator* 11, no. 2 (1980): 30–35.
17. Beyersdorfer, Janet. "Close Encounters of a Junior High Kind." *English Journal* 71 (October 1982): 75–76.
18 Biggs, Alton L. "An Interdisciplinary Course in Big Bend National Park, Texas." *American Biology Teacher* 44 (April 1982): 219–23.
19. Bimes, Beverly J. "Total School Writing: A Working Approach to Writing Problems." *Today's Education* 70 (April-May 1981): 40–41.
20. Blake, Robert W. "How to Talk to a Writer, or Forward to Fundamentals in Teaching Writing." *English Journal* 68 (November 1976): 49–55.

21. Blaya, Jeffrey J. "Say Good-Bye to Those Dumb Old Term Papers." *Audiovisual Instruction* 22 (June-July 1977): 16–18.
22. Boiarsky, Carolyn. "Learning to Write by Writing." *Educational Leadership* 38 (March 1981): 463–64.
23. Bourque, Jane. "Trends in Foreign Language Instruction." *Educational Leadership* 38 (March 1981): 478–81.
24. Brandt, Anthony. "Writing Readiness." *Psychology Today* 16 (March 1982): 55–59.
25. Bredderman, Ted. "What Research Says: Activity Science—the Evidence Shows It Matters." *Science and Children* 20 (September 1982): 39–41.
26. Britton, James. *Language and Learning*. London: Allen Lane, Penguin Press, 1970.
27. Burgess, Carol, et al. *Understanding Children Writing*. Middlesex, Eng.: Penguin Books, 1973.
28. Burmester, David. "Mainstreaming Media: 101 Ways to Use Media in the English Classroom." *English Journal* 72 (February 1983): 109–11.
29. Calkins, Lucy McCormick. "Children Write—and Their Writing Becomes Their Textbook." *Language Arts* 55 (October 1978): 804–10.
30. Calvin, William H., and Ojemann, George A. *Inside the Human Brain*. New York: New American Library, 1980.
31. Camp, Gerald, ed. *Teaching Writing: Essays from the Bay Area Writing Project*. Montclair, N.J.: Boynton/Cook Publishers, 1982.
32. Carlisle, Elizabeth, and Speidel, Judith. "Local History as a Stimulus for Writing." *English Journal* 68 (May 1979): 55–57.
33. Carter, Jack L. "The Human Sciences Program and the Future." *American Biology Teacher* 44 (October 1982): 427–28.
34. Cooper, Charles R., and Odell, Lee. *Research on Composing: Points of Departure*. Urbana, Ill.: National Council of Teachers of English, 1978.
35. Cornell, Joseph Bharat. "Nature: For a Child's Heart and Mind." *Science and Children* 18 (September 1980): 7–13.
36. Cramer, Ronald L. *Children's Writing and Language Growth*. Columbus, Ohio: Charles E. Merrill Publishing Co., 1978.
37. Cribb, Martyn. "Environmental Education, a Subject or Not? Experiences from Hertfordshire." *Bulletin of Environmental Education* 123 (July 1981): 5–7.
38. Danielson, Henry R. "Radio Plays in the Classroom: Another Way to Teach Writing." *English Journal* 70 (October 1981): 84–85.
39. Davis, Lee. "Some Specific Problems." *English Journal* 65 (October 1976): 37–40.
40. Delmar, P. Jay. "Composition and the High School: Steps Toward Faculty-Wide Involvement." *English Journal* 67 (November 1978): 36–38.
41. Detherage, Jim. "Reading, Writing, and Running." *English Journal* 69 (September 1980): 38–41.
42. Dixon, John. *Growth Through English*. London: Oxford University Press for National Association for Teaching of English, 1967.
43. Dommers, John J. "Whales Are Big with Little People." *Humane Education* 5 (December 1981): 2–5.
44. Donlan, Dan. "The Teaching of Writing in the Post-War Years." *English Journal* 68 (April 1979): 73–78.
45. Dunwoody, Sharon. "From a Journalist's Perspective: Putting Content into Mass Media Science Writing." *English Journal* 67 (April 1978): 44–47.

46. Elbow, Peter. *Writing Without Teachers.* New York: Oxford University Press, 1973.
47. Ellman, Neil. "The Two Cultures: Exploring and Bridging the Gap." *English Journal* 65 (October 1976): 55–56.
48. Emig, Janet. *The Composing Processes of Twelfth Graders.* Urbana, Ill.: National Council of Teachers of English, 1971.
49. English, David A. "With Grammar on My Left: English Teaching and the Second World War." *English Journal* 68 (April 1979): 67–72.
50. Enke, C. G. "Scientific Writing: One Scientist's Perspective." *English Journal* 67 (April 1978): 40–43.
51. Engdahl, Sylvia. "Do Teenage Novels Fill a Need?" *English Journal* 64 (February 1975): 48–52.
52. Estus, Charles, et al. "An Interdisciplinary Approach to Community Studies." *History Teacher* 13 (November 1979): 37–48.
53. Evertts, Eldonna L. *Explorations in Children's Writing.* Urbana, Ill.: National Council of Teachers of English, 1970.
54. Falk, Julia. "Language Acquisition and the Teaching and Learning of Writing." *College English* 41 (December 1979): 436–47.
55. Fien, John. "Values Probing: An Integrated Approach to Values Education in Geography." *Journal of Geography* 80 (January 1981): 19–22.
56. Florio, Susan. "The Problem of Dead Letters: Social Perspectives on the Teaching of Writing. *Elementary School Journal* 80 (September 1979): 1–7.
57. Fowler, John M., and Carey, Helen H. "Energy and Social Studies—a Match That Works." *Social Studies* 71 (March–April 1980): 56–60.
58. Fulwiler, Toby. "Journals Across the Curriculum." *English Journal* 69 (December 1980): 14–19.
59. ————, and Young, Art. *Language Connections: Writing and Reading Across the Curriculum.* Urbana, Ill.: National Council of Teachers of English, 1982.
60. Gennaro, Eugene, and Heller, Patricia. "Early Adolescence: Out-of-School Science Experiences." *Science and Children* 20 (September 1982): 22–23.
61. Geschwind, Norman. "Specializations of the Human Brain." *Scientific American* 241 (September 1979): 180–99.
62. Gonzalez, Roseann Duenas. "Teaching Mexican-American Students to Write: Capitalizing on the Culture." *English Journal* 71 (November 1982): 20–24.
63. Graves, Donald. "An Examination of the Writing Processes of Seven-Year-Old Children." *Research in the Teaching of English* 9 (Winter 1975): 227–41.
64. ————. *Writing: Children at Work.* Exeter, N.H.: Heinemann Publishers, 1982.
65. Greenberg, Arthur. "City-as-School: An Approach to External Interdisciplinary Education." *English Journal* 65 (October 1976): 60–62.
66. Greene, Joyce G. "Broadening the Scope of Biology Education." *American Biology Teacher* 39 (November 1977): 491–94.
67. Grinstein, Louise S. "A Subject Classification of Math Lab Activities from *School Science and Mathematics." School Science and Mathematics* 82 (November 1982): 573–75.
68. Hairston, Maxine. "The Winds of Change: Thomas Kuhn and the Revolution in the Teaching of Writing." *College Composition and Communication* 33 (February 1982): 76–87.
69. Halpern, Jeanne H., and Mathews, Dale. "Helping Inexperienced

Writers: An Informal Discussion with Mina Shaughnessy." *English Journal* 63 (March 1980): 32–37.

70. Hamilton, Dorothy G. "Using Fine Arts to Teach Science." *Science and Children* 19 (September 1981): 6–10.

71. Harris, Heather. " 'Neglected Heritage'—The 'Whys' and 'Hows' of Developing a Sport History School Program." *History and Social Science Teacher* 17 (September 1982): 171–74.

72. Harris, Janet A. "Chemically Speaking . . . Who Done It?" *Science Teacher* 49 (September 1982): 42–44.

73. Hart, Leslie. "Brain-Compatible Teaching." *Today's Education* 67 (November–December 1978): 42, 45.

74. Herrington, Anne J. "Writing to Learn: Writing Across the Disciplines." *College English* 43 (April 1981): 379–87.

75. Hipple, Theodore W., et al. "Forty-Plus Writing Activities." *English Journal* (March 1983): 73–76.

76. Hofstein, Avi, and Yager, Robert E. "Science Education Attuned to Social Issues: Challenges for the 80's." *Science Teacher* 48 (December 1981): 12–14.

77. Huidekoper, Peter, Jr. "My Russian Literature Class—the Good News." *English Journal* 72 (January 1983): 42–45.

78. Hurst, Donna. "Our Solar System Invades the Classroom." *Instructor* 89 (February 1980): 72.

79. Jacobsen, Mary. "Students Write Stories: Inside-Out and Inside-In. *English Quarterly* 14 (Winter 1981–82): 41–48.

80. Jensen, Mary. "Alternatives for Outdoor Education Programming." *Journal of Physical Education and Recreation* 52 (October 1981): 64–67.

81. Johnson, Marvin. "Writing in Mathematics Classes: A Valuable Tool for Learning." *Mathematics Teacher* 76 (February 1983): 117–19.

82. Judy, Stephen N. "Writing for the Here and Now: An Approach to Assessing Student Writing." *English Journal* 62 (January 1973): 69–79.

83. _____. *The ABC's of Literacy: A Guide for Parents and Teachers.* New York: Oxford University Press, 1980.

84. _____, ed. *Reading.* P.O. Box 895, Rochester, Mich.: Michigan Council of Teachers of English, 1980.

85. _____, and Susan. *The English Teacher's Handbook: Ideas and Resources for Teaching English.* Cambridge: Winthrop Publishers, 1979.

86. Kahn, Norma B. "Proposal for Motivating More Students to Lifetime Reading of Literature." *English Journal* 63 (February 1974): 34–43.

87. Kantor, Kenneth J. "Research in Composition: What It Means for Teachers." *English Journal* (February 1981): 64–67.

88. Kendig, Frank. "A Conversation with Roger Schank." *Psychology Today* 17 (April 1983): 28–36.

89. Kimball, Daniel B. "Social Studies in the Rough: Students Hike in the High Sierras." *Today's Education* 70 (February–March 1981): 39–40.

90. Kimmel, Howard. "Energy Topics in the Mathematics Classroom." *School Science and Mathematics* 82 (April 1982): 273–78.

91. Klasky, Charles. "World Geography—Believe It or Not!" *Social Education* 43 (January 1979): 34–35.

92. Kohl, Herbert. *Basic Skills.* Boston: Little Brown, 1982.

93. La Rocque, Geraldine E. "You Gotta Kiss a Lotta Frogs Before You Find Prince Charming." *English Journal* 68 (December 1979): 31–35.

94. Lassen, N.; Ingvar, D.; and Skinhj, E. "Brain Function and Blood Flow." *Scientific American* 239 (October 1978): 62–71.

95. Leake, Lowell. "What Every Secondary School Mathematics Teacher Should Read—Twenty-Four Option." *Mathematics Teacher* 76 (February 1983): 128–32.
96. Lehr, Fran. "ERIC/RCS Report: Writing as Learning in the Content Areas." *English Journal* 69 (November 1980): 23–25.
97. Leon, Warren. "Using History Museums." *New English Social Studies Bulletin* 37 (September 1980): 27.
98. Lewis, Melanie. "Observing the Environment Through Art." *Science and Children* 19 (September 1981): 11–12.
99. Lewis, William. "Two Technical Writing Assignments." *English Journal* 67 (April 1978): 65–67.
100. Licata, Kenneth. "Writing Is Part of Literacy, Too!" *Science Teacher* 47 (February 1980): 124–26.
101. Lotto, Edward, and Smith, Bruce. "Making Grading Work." *College English* 41 (December 1979): 423–31.
102. Lundsteen, Sara W., ed. *Help for the Teacher of Written Composition.* Urbana, Ill.: ERIC, 1976.
103. McClure, Tim. "Becoming Part of the News." *English Journal* 71 (December 1982): 45–46.
104. McLeod, Alan. "Stimulating Writing Through Job Awareness." *English Journal* 67 (November 1978): 42–43.
105. Magelli, Paul J. "Language: The Problems, the Promise." *Hispania* 64 (March 1981): 68–72.
106. Marcus, Stephen. "Any Teacher a Writing Teacher? The Value of 'Free Writing.'" *Improving College and University Teaching* 28 (Winter 1980): 10–12.
107. Markle, Sandra. "Super Science Send-Homes." *Instructor* 92 (October 1982): 51–56.
108. Martin, Nancy. *Writing and Learning Across the Curriculum.* Montclair, N.J.: Boynton/Cook Publishers, 1976.
109. Maxwell, Rhoda, and Judy, Stephen. "Science Writing in the English Classroom: *English Journal* Workshop." *English Journal* 67 (April 1978): 78–81.
110. _____, and _____. *Evaluating a Theme.* P.O. Box 895, Rochester, Mich.: Michigan Council of Teachers of English, 1981.
111. Metcalf, James. "Teaching Writing in Physical Education and Recreation." *Journal of Physical Education and Recreation* 50 (November–December 1979): 38.
112. Moffett, James. *Active Voice: A Writing Program Across the Curriculum.* Montclair, N.J.: Boynton/Cook Publishers, 1981.
113. Moskowitz, Arlene. "The Acquisition of Langauge." *Scientific American* 239 (November 1978): 92–108.
114. Moskowitz, Gertrude. "Effects of Humanistic Techniques on Attitude, Cohesiveness, and Self-Concept of Foreign Language Students." *Modern Language Journal* 65 (Summer 1981): 149–57.
115. Murray, Donald M. "Why Teach Writing—and How?" *English Journal* 62 (December 1973): 1234–37.
116. _____. "Teach the Motivating Force of Revision." *English Journal* 67 (October 1978): 56–60.
117. Neidich, Carole Louise. "Learning on Skis." *Outdoor Communicator* 11, no. 2 (1980): 21–27.
118. Norby, Shirley. "Myths, Mummies, and Museums." *School Arts* 78 (April 1979): 21.
119. Nord, James R. "Developing Listening Fluency Before Speaking: An Alternative Paradigm." Paper presented at the Fifth World Congress of Applied Linguistics, University of Montreal, Montreal, Quebec, Canada. August 25, 1978.

120. Northcroft, David. "Pupils' Writing: Product, Process, and Evaluation." *English in Education* 13 (Summer 1979): 7–18.
121. Odell, Lee. "The Process of Writing and the Process of Learning." *College Composition and Communication* 31 (February 1980): 42–50.
122. Olson, D. R., and Bruner, J. S. "Learning Through Experience and Learning Through Media." In *Media and Symbols: The Forms of Expression, Communication and Education,* edited by D. R. Olson. Chicago, Ill.: University of Chicago Press, 1971.
123. Page, Dorothy H. "Yankee Doodle Noodle Company Needs You." *Teacher* 95 (February 1978): 82–92.
124. Patrick, John, and Remy, Richard C. "Crossing Two Cultures in the Education of Citizens." *American Biology Teacher.* 44 (September 1982): 346–50.
125. Pereira-Mendoza, Lionel, and May, Sadie. "The Environment—a Teaching Aid." *School Science and Mathematics* 83 (January 1983): 54–60.
126. Pescatello, Ann. "Humanists in the Schools." *Social Studies Review* 21 (Winter 1982): 53–55.
127. Petry, Karla L. *"La Chanson de Roland* in the Elementary School Classroom: A Case for Medieval Literature and Young Language Students." *Modern Language Journal* 65 (Summer 1981): 137–40.
128. Picker, Les. "What Is Marine Education?" *Science and Children* 18 (October 1980): 10–11.
129. Pontin, R. G., and Thomson, I. "A Thematic Approach to the Teaching of Physics." *Physics Education* 16 (May 1981): 167–72.
130. Pytlik, Edward C. "Technology Education and Human Values: A Course for High School Students." *Journal of Epsilon Pi Tau* 7 (Fall 1981): 36–43.
131. Rizzolo, Patricia. "Peer Tutors Make Good Teachers: A Successful Writing Program." *Improving College and University Teaching* 30 (Summer 1982): 115–19.
132. Rosen, Connie and Rosen, Harold. *The Language of Primary School Children.* Middlesex, England: Penguin Books, 1973.
133. Rosenblatt, Louise M. *Literature as Exploration.* New York: Noble and Noble, Publishers, 1976.
134. Rosenthal, Dorothy B. "A 'Science and Society' Course for High School Students." *American Biology Teacher* 41 (September 1979): 336–40.
135. Routtenberg, Aryeh. "The Reward System of the Brain." *Scientific American* 239 (November 1978): 154–64.
136. Safane, Clifford. "Music for Everyone." *Teachers and Writers* 9 (Spring 1978): 29–33.
137. Salz, Arthur E. "Score a Curriculum Victory with Sports." *Instructor* 89 (March 1980): 62–64.
138. Schick, James B. "Using the Microfilmed *Virginia Gazette* in Class." *History Teacher* 13 (February 1980): 223–38.
139. Shadiow, Linda. "Every Teacher as a Writing Teacher: A Definition of Terms." *NASSP Bulletin* 65 (April 1981): 47–53.
140. Shaughnessy, Mina. *Errors and Expectations: A Guide for the Teacher of Basic Writing.* New York: Oxford University Press, 1977.
141. Smith, Frank. *Comprehension and Learning: A Conceptual Framework for Teachers.* New York: Holt, Rinehart and Winston, 1975.
142. Smith, Vernon. "Beyond Flax and Skinner: A Personal Perspective on Teaching English." *English Journal* 68 (April 1979): 79–85.
143. Snyder, Kathleen, and Palay, Carol P. "Teaming English and Social Studies: An American Civilization Experience." *History Teacher* 15 (February 1982): 197–206.
144. Soler, Francisco de P., and Schuster, Richard E. "Compound Growth

and Related Situations: A Problem-Solving Approach." *Mathematics Teacher* 75 (November 1982): 640–44.

145. Springer, Mark A. "The Role of Science in the English Class." *English Journal* 65 (October 1976): 35–36.

146. Stangl, Jean. "No-Cook Cookery. Forty-five Delicious Learning Activities Based on a Topic All Kids Love—Food!" *Instructor* 92 (October 1982): 40–42.

147. Stein, Harry. "Ivan the Terrible Writes His Resume." *Instructor* 92 (October 1982): 46–50.

148. Sunderland, Harold. "The Arts and Humanities in the 1981 History/Social Science Framework." *Social Studies Review* 21 (Fall 1981): 26–30.

149. Swift, Jonathan. "Global Education: What's in It for Us?" *English Journal* 69 (December 1980): 46–50.

150. Switzer, Thomas, and Burton, Voss. "Integrating the Teaching of Science and Social Studies." *School Science and Mathematics* 82 (October 1982): 452–62.

151. Tchudi, Stephen N., and Tchudi, Susan J. *Teaching Writing in the Content Areas: Elementary School.* Washington, D.C.: National Education Association, 1983.

152. ———, and Huerta, Margie C. *Teaching Writing in the Content Areas: Middle School/Junior High.* Washington, D.C.: National Education Association, 1983.

153. ———, and Yates, Joanne. *Teaching Writing in the Content Areas: Senior High School.* Washington, D.C.: National Education Association, 1983.

154. Toothaker, Roy E. "Getting Kids to Write About Science." *Instructor* 90 (November 1980): 120, 124.

155. Troutman, Benjamin I. "Interdisciplinary English: Methods and Materials." *English Journal* 65 (October 1976): 49–52.

156. Tschumy, Ruth D. "Writing Across the Curriculum—What's in a Name?" *NASSP Bulletin* 46 (May 1982): 63–70.

157. Tunning, William A. "Olympic Games: An Interdisciplinary Model." *Journal of Physical Education and Recreation.* 52 (April 1981): 72–73.

158. Veit, Richard C. "De-Grading Composition: Do Papers Need Grades?" *College English* 41 (December 1979): 432–35.

159. Vollmer, Gerard W. "Science Lore in the Old Farmer's Almanac." *Science Teacher* 47 (December 1980): 34.

160. Wagner, Eileen N. "How to Avoid Grading Compositions." *English Journal* 68 (March 1979): 76–79.

161. Warren, Barbara Leonard. "Of Bags and Boxes: How to Banish the Book Report Without Getting Fired." *English Journal* 66 (February 1977): 70–73.

162. Watson, F. R. "Mathematics Teacher Education Project: Links with the Educational Disciplines." *Journal of Education for Teaching* 8 (January 1982): 14–20.

163. Weingartner, Charles. "Getting to Some Basics that the Back-to-Basics-Movement Doesn't Get To." *English Journal* 66 (October 1977): 39–44.

164. Wirtz, Ruth E. "The Center Spot: Safari Schoolroom." *Teacher* 97 (April 1980): 20–24.

165. Zipko, Stephen J. "An Interdisciplinary Approach to Dinosaur Fossils, Morphology, Ethology, and Energetics." *American Biology Teacher* 43 (November 1981): 430–39.

166. Zoller, Uri, and Weiss, Shoshana. "'Hashish and Marijuana'—An Innovative Interdisciplinary Drug Education Curricular Program for High Schools." *Journal of Drug Education* 11, no. 1 (1981): 37–46.